Original title:
Chasing Shadows in a Sunlit Mind

Copyright © 2024 Creative Arts Management OÜ
All rights reserved.

Author: Gideon Shaw
ISBN HARDBACK: 978-9916-90-584-5
ISBN PAPERBACK: 978-9916-90-585-2

Sunkissed Echoes of the Mind's Terrain

In fields where sunlight plays,
Thoughts drift like whispers soft,
Memories dance in golden rays,
Painting shadows, dreams aloft.

The heart's canvas, warm and bright,
Brushstrokes of a summer's day,
Each moment glimmers with delight,
As echoes of laughter sway.

Beneath the sky, vast and clear,
A tapestry of fleeting time,
Sunkissed moments drawing near,
In harmony, they softly chime.

So pause and breathe the gentle air,
Let the echoes guide your way,
In the sunlight, cast your care,
Embrace each dawn, cherish the play.

Traces of Wonder in the Palette of Daylight

In the morning's gentle hue,
Colors blend in soft embrace,
Nature hums a tune so true,
A masterpiece in open space.

Brushes dipped in azure skies,
Each stroke a tale yet untold,
Through emerald paths, the heart flies,
As warmth of sunlight turns to gold.

With every step, the world ignites,
A symphony of sights and sounds,
In wonder's heart, pure delight,
Where beauty in stillness abounds.

The canvas breathes, alive and free,
Traces of magic fill the air,
In daylight's glow, we will see,
The art of living, rich and rare.

Hidden Faces Beneath a Bright Sky

Amidst the clouds, secrets hide,
Whispers of dreams drift far and wide.
Below the sun's warm golden gaze,
Shadows of souls lost in the haze.

Each smile a mask, each laugh a lie,
Beneath the light, the quiet sigh.
In the dance of warmth, hearts collide,
Yet hidden truths are deep inside.

Reflections of Illusions in Daylight

Mirrors glimmer with tales untold,
Truth and fiction, a web of gold.
In bright beams, they weave and sway,
Dancing echoes of a fleeting day.

Fragments shimmer, like glass in light,
Life's canvas painted, dark and bright.
Moments captured, yet lost in time,
Illusions twist, a silent rhyme.

In the Garden of Glimmering Hues

Petals flutter in vibrant song,
Nature's palette where dreams belong.
Colors blend in a fragrant air,
Whispers soft, love's gentle care.

Beneath each leaf, stories grow,
In every shadow, a secret flow.
Dewdrops glisten in morning's light,
A garden's heart, pure and bright.

Flickers in the Canvas of Thought

Ideas spark like fireflies bright,
In the dark, they dance with delight.
Canvas stretched, with colors bold,
Every stroke tells more than told.

Thoughts intertwine in a vivid play,
A tapestry woven, night and day.
In the silence of the mind's own space,
Flickers of genius leave a trace.

Streaks of Light Across a Wandering Mind

In shadows deep, where thoughts take flight,
Streaks of light cut through the night.
Whispers dance in endless streams,
Illuminating forgotten dreams.

Across the canvas of my soul,
Fragments gather, making whole.
Ephemeral visions merge and blend,
In fleeting moments, I transcend.

The Lure of Light in a Shimmering Mindscape

In shimmering hues, the mind unwinds,
The lure of light, where hope confides.
Each glimmer calls, a siren's song,
In this vast landscape, I belong.

The colors swirl, a vibrant sea,
A dance of thoughts, wild and free.
Within the glow, I chase the trace,
Of dreams that time cannot erase.

Dreamers Among the Glimmering Rays

Dreamers wander, hearts alight,
Among the rays that pierce the night.
In every glow, a story's spun,
A tapestry of dreams begun.

Together we chase the fleeting gleam,
In a world where shadows seem.
Our hopes rise high, like birds in flight,
Transcending darkness, reaching light.

Fragments of Time in Golden Glow

Fragments of time in golden glow,
Remind us where our spirits flow.
Every moment, a piece of art,
Captured softly within the heart.

As twilight fades, memories gleam,
Reflecting life, like a tender dream.
In the silence, echoes sing,
Of fleeting joys that time will bring.

Ephemeral Dreams at Dawn

In the hush of morning's light,
Dreams dissolve in soft delight.
Silhouettes of yesterday,
Fade as night slips far away.

Whispers linger in the air,
Fleeting visions, pure and rare.
Chasing echoes of the night,
As daybreak steals the stars from sight.

The Light's Elusive Dance

Sunlight filters through the trees,
Nature sways with gentle breeze.
Shadows play and flicker bright,
  A ballet of day and night.

Twirling beams in golden hues,
Softly casting wandering views.
Every moment, brief and clear,
  Capturing both joy and fear.

Whispers of Light and Shade

In the twilight's soft embrace,
Secrets hide, a hidden place.
Flickering flames, shadows grin,
Echoes of what lies within.

Crickets sing in evening's glow,
Underneath the stars' soft flow.
Whispers drift on evening's air,
Intertwining hope and despair.

Pursuit of Flickering Thoughts

Thoughts chase like fireflies at dusk,
Evasive, fleeting, wrapped in musk.
Captured in a moment's grace,
Dancing in the mind's embrace.

Fragile like the morning dew,
Each idea feels fresh and new.
Pursuing shadows, bright and fleet,
In the dark, they find their beat.

Fleeting Glimmers of Forgotten Tales

In shadows where whispers softly play,
Old stories linger, then drift away.
Stars blink gently, a moment's grace,
Each memory held in time's embrace.

Echoes of laughter, faint and thin,
Ghosts of the past, where dreams begin.
Through streets of silence, we wander alone,
In fleeting glimmers, the heart finds home.

Navigating the Labyrinth of Luminescence

Through twisting paths of radiant light,
We chase the shadows, our fears ignited.
Each turn unveils a mystery bright,
Guided by stars in the velvet night.

Whispers in twilight, soft as a sigh,
They beckon us onward, through the night sky.
In the maze of dreams, we lose our way,
Yet find our truth in the dawn's first ray.

Light's Silent Retreat

When daylight dims, the world holds breath,
In silence blooms a dance with death.
Shadows stretch long, as twilight sighs,
A canvas painted with starlit lies.

Softly the moon drapes silver threads,
Weaving through thoughts as daylight sheds.
In night's embrace, where secrets hide,
Light takes its leave, with no place to bide.

The Spectrum of a Wandering Mind

Thoughts cascade like a rainbow's bend,
Coloring moments, they twist and blend.
Fleeting shades of joy and despair,
A tapestry woven in the silent air.

From dreams that flicker, to fears that bloom,
Each hue a whisper, each shade a room.
As the mind wanders, it drifts afar,
Finding solace beneath a distant star.

Luminous Whispers of Yesterday

In twilight's glow, the secrets hum,
Soft echoes of a time begun.
The fading stars, they softly weep,
For memories we strive to keep.

Amidst the haze of shadowed light,
Fleeting dreams take graceful flight.
Each whisper, like a gentle sigh,
Reminds us of the days gone by.

Veils of Brightness and Shade

Within the dance of dusk and dawn,
Colors blend, and fears are drawn.
A canvas painted with pure grace,
  Illuminates the hidden face.

With every beam that breaks the night,
  Veils of shadows hide the light.
Yet in the depths, hope softly glows,
Through every trial, a path still shows.

The Pursuit of Radiant Phantoms

Chasing ghosts of brilliant dreams,
Through tangled paths and silver beams.
We run, we leap, towards the bright,
The phantoms fade in morning light.

Yet still we seek, our hearts aflame,
For each moment, we'll reclaim.
The shimmering threads that bind us tight,
In whispers of the starry night.

Gathering Light from the Edge of Dreams

From distant realms, a glow unfolds,
Stories waiting to be told.
In every flicker, hope resides,
As destiny and courage ride.

We gather shards of twilight's grace,
In every lost and cherished place.
With open hearts and hands outstretched,
We weave the dreams that life has etched.

Flickering Thoughts in the Realm of Day

In the morning's gentle glow,
Ideas dance like shadows low.
Whispers float on breezes light,
Fleeting moments take their flight.

A canvas bright with colors bold,
Stories waiting to be told.
Each thought a spark within the air,
A flicker here, a flicker there.

Captured dreams in sunlight's beam,
Awakening from a silent theme.
Yet the day begins to wane,
As thoughts flicker like summer rain.

In twilight's calm, they softly sway,
Carried gently, far away.
A realm where visions come to play,
In flickering thoughts of day.

Echoes of Luminous Longing

Beneath the stars, a soft refrain,
Whispers of what might remain.
Brushed by dreams of silver hue,
Searching for a love so true.

The night unfolds with sparkling lights,
Echoing hopes in quiet flights.
In shadows deep, the heart will yearn,
For warmth and light that brightly burn.

Each heartbeat sings a distant song,
Resonating where we belong.
Luminous paths that intertwine,
In echoes soft, our souls align.

As dawn breaks through the velvet sky,
Longing whispers a gentle sigh.
Yet within the golden glow,
The echoes of love still flow.

Patterns of Light on the Canvas of Dream

In dreams we find a world anew,
Painted skies in shades of blue.
Patterns forming, bright and clear,
A tapestry of hope so near.

Brushstrokes of a vivid past,
Moments fleeting, shadows cast.
Each vision glimmers in the night,
Awakens in the softest light.

A dance of colors, bold and free,
Whirling through a memory.
Reflections captured, lost in thought,
In this canvas, battles fought.

As dawn approaches, dreams abide,
In hearts where secrets still reside.
Patterns glowing in sweet embrace,
On the canvas of time and space.

Sunlit Mysteries in a Curious Mind

Curious thoughts in sunlit gleam,
Unravel truth from tangled dream.
A quest for wonders, vast and bright,
In shadows deep, a spark of light.

What lies beyond the horizon's edge?
Secrets whispered with a pledge.
Each moment holds a treasure's key,
Unlocking paths we yearn to see.

In solitude, the mind takes flight,
Chasing whispers through the night.
Sunlit mysteries softly chime,
Echoes captured, lost in time.

With every glance, a question's born,
In quiet moments, hope reborn.
A curious heart will ever find,
Sunlit mysteries in the mind.

The Search for Traces in Golden Rays

In the meadow where shadows play,
Whispers follow the light of day.
Footprints linger on paths once trod,
Leaving secrets beneath the nod.

Golden rays kiss the earth's soft skin,
A treasure hunt that begins within.
Each glimmer holds a tale untold,
A longing for the brave and bold.

Searching in corners where memories blend,
With every breeze, the echoes send.
The dance of light, a guiding thread,
In the search for traces, hope is spread.

As twilight falls and shadows creep,
The golden rays, a promise to keep.
In their warmth, we find our way,
To the heart of dreams, to contented stay.

Blossoms of Imagination Under the Sun

Beneath the bright and shining dome,
Ideas bloom, far away from home.
Petals of thought in vibrant hues,
Nurtured by the sunlight's muse.

Each blossom tells a story grand,
A world shaped by a gentle hand.
Whispers float on the summer breeze,
In every heart, the spirit frees.

With every spark, a vision ignites,
A canvas painted with pure delights.
Imagination's dance, a joyful spin,
Where dreams take root and magic begins.

Under the sun, we chase our grace,
Finding hope in a sacred space.
In this garden, wild and free,
Blossoms of thought, our legacy.

Reveries and Radiance in the Journey of Mind

In the realm where thoughts unfold,
Light beams out, a treasure of gold.
Reveries drift between the stars,
Where dreams escape their earthly bars.

The journey is wrought with twists unseen,
In the landscape of what might have been.
Radiance flows through winding paths,
A tapestry spun with heart's warm laughs.

Each step reveals a truth profound,
In silence, echoes of joy resound.
With every heartbeat, we explore,
The wonders held behind mind's door.

With twilight's grace, the vision glows,
In the warmth of all that life bestows.
In reveries bright, we pave the way,
To a future woven with dreams today.

Sunlit Reflections in the Pool of Dreams

In the stillness of the morning light,
Reflecting worlds, calm and bright.
Ripples dance on the surface clear,
In the pool of dreams, hopes draw near.

Sunlit reflections, a gentle sway,
Whispering secrets of the day.
Each wave a memory, softly spun,
In the silence, a journey begun.

Glimmers shimmer like stars that fall,
In their beauty, we hear the call.
The depths hold treasures, deep and vast,
Moments cherished, shadows cast.

As day fades into a twilight hue,
The pool mirrors all we ever knew.
In every dream, a chance to find,
New paths woven, soul aligned.

Radiance Stretched Across the Horizon

Sunrise dances on the sea,
Painting skies in hues so free.
Each ray whispers a gentle tale,
Of distant dreams upon the gale.

Mountains crown the waking land,
Casting shadows, bold and grand.
Golden light, the world ignites,
Chasing away the lingering nights.

The horizon wakes with a sigh,
Awakening spirits, soaring high.
In this moment, breath is caught,
Embracing all, yet seeking naught.

As daylight stretches wide in space,
We find our place in nature's grace.
With each heartbeat, joy unfolds,
In this radiance, life beholds.

Pastel Illustrations of Fleeting Fantasies

In soft hues, the dreams collide,
Pastel worlds where hopes abide.
Whispers paint the air with grace,
Fleeting moments we embrace.

Clouds like candy, drifting by,
Fragrant flowers in the sky.
Each thought fluttering, light and sweet,
In this magic, time's heartbeat.

Sketches float on gentle streams,
Paper boats with vibrant seams.
Childlike laughter fills the air,
As fantasies lay hidden there.

With every stroke, our minds take flight,
Creating visions filled with light.
In these drawings of the mind,
Pastel hopes, forever kind.

Vistas of Light in the Garden of Reflection

Amidst the blooms, the sunlight weaves,
Casting shadows beneath the leaves.
Mirrored petals catch the gleam,
In this garden, find your dream.

Rippling waters softly sing,
Every ripple, a secret spring.
Reflecting thoughts that gently sway,
In this haven, pause to stay.

Butterflies dance, a fleeting show,
Colors blend, a radiant glow.
As the twilight starts to fall,
Nature's whispers softly call.

Harvest peace from every sight,
In the garden, bask in light.
Let reflections guide the way,
Finding solace in the day.

A Fluttering Heart Beneath the Helm of Daylight

Beneath the sun, a heart awakes,
In gentle warmth, the spirit shakes.
Each beat echoes in the dawn,
From shadows deep, we're gently drawn.

With every ray, the world ignites,
In vibrant hues, our hope takes flight.
fluttering dreams take center stage,
As passions bloom, we turn the page.

In daylight's grasp, we learn to see,
The magic woven in the free.
Moments captured in a glance,
In this embrace, we find our dance.

Let the heart beneath the sun,
Be a beacon, never done.
Through every trial, every plight,
A fluttering soul in the light.

Frayed Edges of Daylight's Dream

In twilight glow, the shadows play,
A dance of whispers, soft and stray.
The stars awake, their secrets loom,
In this brief pause, the night finds room.

The colors fade, but hearts ignite,
With woven hopes, we chase the light.
As dreams unfold, we drift anew,
In fragile threads, our spirits grew.

The dawn breaks forth, a canvas wide,
Painting the sky with hues of pride.
Yet in these frayed and fleeting beams,
We find the path that leads to dreams.

So let us wander, hand in hand,
Through daylight's breath, the golden sand.
For every end, a start appears,
In frayed edges, we conquer fears.

The Fragrance of Light in Untamed Thoughts

A whispering breeze through the tall green grass,
The sunlight dances, as moments pass.
In thoughts untamed, we seek the truth,
Like flowers wild, we reclaim our youth.

The fragrance lingers, sweet and bright,
With every breath, we reach for light.
An echo of laughter, a soft refrain,
In the heart's garden, joy shall remain.

As shadows stretch and day succumbs,
The moon reveals what silence hums.
With open minds, we forge our way,
In untamed thoughts, we boldly stray.

So let us wander where colors burst,
In the fragrance of light, we quench our thirst.
For every moment, a chance to see,
In this wild world, we shall be free.

Shimmering Visions Beyond the Gloom

In corners dark, a flicker glows,
Whispering secrets, nobody knows.
A shimmer breaks the silent night,
With visions clear, our souls take flight.

Beyond the clouds, where hopes arise,
The dawn unveils, a clear blue skies.
Each radiant beam, a guiding star,
In shimmering dreams, we've come so far.

Though shadows linger, and fears may creep,
Within our hearts, the light runs deep.
We chase the spark that keeps us whole,
Through shimmering visions, we find our soul.

So let us dance where light will lead,
With every step, we plant the seed.
For beyond the gloom, the path is bright,
In shimmering visions, we'll find our light.

Veils of Thought Beneath the Bright Celestial

Beneath the stars, we weave our dreams,
In veils of thought, the cosmos streams.
Each question posed, a mystery spun,
In the night's embrace, the journey's begun.

Threads of wonder, tangled and free,
Connect us all, like waves in the sea.
Through veils of thought, our spirits soar,
Beyond the bounds of evermore.

With every pulse of distant light,
We glimpse the truth, both bold and bright.
In the vastness where ideas collide,
Veils of thought become our guide.

So let's explore these realms unknown,
In every heart, seeds of light are sown.
For beneath the celestial's gaze so grand,
Our veils of thought will take their stand.

Pursuit of Fleeting Dreams

Chasing whispers in the night,
Where shadows softly weave.
A dance of hope, a fragile light,
In hearts that dare believe.

Through valleys deep where silence lies,
We search for what is lost.
Each sigh a wish, each tear a prize,
In dreams, we pay the cost.

Moments slip like grains of sand,
Yet still we reach with grace.
With open hearts and outstretched hands,
We long to find our place.

In the twilight, whispers fade,
Yet courage lifts us high.
For in the dark, our hopes invade,
And paint the starlit sky.

Daydreams Amidst the Sunlit Shade

Beneath the boughs where breezes play,
I drift in gentle thought.
The world may melt, then fade away,
Yet solace here is sought.

Golden light like honey flows,
On petals, soft and bright.
In every bloom, a wonder grows,
Awakening pure delight.

With every sigh, the moment sways,
The mind begins to roam.
In daydreams lost, I find my ways,
To call this place my home.

The hour slips but leaves a trace,
Of whimsy wrapped in gold.
In sunlit thoughts, I find my grace,
Amidst the warmest fold.

Elusive Visions in the Wake of Radiance

In morning's light, like dreams take flight,
A shimmer at the dawn.
Elusive forms, so bright, so slight,
They beckon, then are gone.

I chase the glow through fields of white,
Where visions come alive.
With every step, a spark ignites,
A truth that starts to thrive.

Yet shadows loom, and time does bend,
As echoes start to fade.
In every chase, an unseen end,
Where hopes and fears parade.

But still I seek that fleeting dream,
In every sunlit ray.
For in the heart, a vibrant gleam,
Can never quite decay.

Fading Forms Under the Azure Sphere

Beneath the vast and azure sky,
I watch the shadows drift.
Like whispered thoughts that fade nearby,
In silence, they uplift.

Soft echoes of a time once known,
Where laughter filled the air.
Now fading forms, like seeds are sown,
To linger, light and rare.

With every breath, I sense the change,
The world in constant flow.
In colors bright, both bold and strange,
The moments come and go.

Yet still I gather every thread,
Of beauty, lost but near.
In fading forms, where dreams are fed,
Resilience blooms, sincere.

Threads of Light Through the Mist

In the morning hush, soft gleams arise,
Threads of silver weave through the skies,
Whispers of dawn in the gentle dance,
Misty shadows fade, caught in a trance.

Nature's canvas draped in a veil,
Glistening beams tell a timeless tale,
Each flicker a promise, a secret to share,
Guiding the lost with a tender care.

Branches stretch out to embrace the day,
Light filters softly, in vibrant play,
Each moment a treasure, a fleeting sight,
Crafted with love, threads of pure light.

As the sun climbs high, the world awakes,
Radiant paths where the heart partakes,
In every breath, in every sigh,
Threads of light linger, as dreams soar high.

Enigmatic Glows in the Calm

In the stillness of dusk, soft glows emerge,
Whispers of evening in shadows converge,
Mystic hues paint the vast open sky,
As stars twinkle softly, like dreams passing by.

Beneath the quiet, secrets unfold,
Enigmatic stories of warmth and of cold,
Each shimmer a hint of the infinite deep,
A lullaby beckoning the night into sleep.

River's soft murmur, a gentle refrain,
Reflects the light in a warm, soothing vein,
With every pulse, with every sigh,
The calm envelopes, as time drifts by.

In the cool embrace of the night's gentle hand,
The glows invite wonder, as dreams brightly stand,
Enigmatic moments, forever to hold,
In the haven of night, where stories unfold.

Whispers in the Golden Light

Through the leaves of autumn, gold glimmers bright,
Whispers of warmth in the softening light,
A dance of the breeze with the fading year,
Tender reflections, where nothing is clear.

Sunset unfolds in a soft, warm embrace,
Kissing the earth with a delicate grace,
Echoes of laughter in russet and red,
Painting the moments that linger, unsaid.

With each step forward, the world slows down,
Golden whispers gather, with no time to frown,
Blessings of twilight, a melody sweet,
Stirring the heart to a soft, steady beat.

In the hush of the dusk, the magic unveils,
Whispers of hope as the daylight pales,
In golden light, every shadow takes flight,
Embracing the silence, a beautiful sight.

Ephemeral Footprints on a Dazzling Day

Footprints in sand, fleeting and bright,
Carved by the waves, kissed by the light,
Each step a story of laughter and play,
Ephemeral moments that fade away.

The sky is a canvas with colors untold,
Dazzling the heart, like treasures to hold,
Sunbeams and laughter, a whimsical sway,
Chasing the shadows, come what may.

Time drifts like clouds, soft and serene,
Gentle reminders of what could have been,
As footprints dissolve in the tide's gentle hold,
Stories of joy that remain ever bold.

In the warmth of the sun, life dances and spins,
Ephemeral treasures where everything begins,
A dazzling day, a fleeting ballet,
Carving our dreams in the sand, then away.

Sunbeams and Elusive Figures

In the morning light they dance,
Softly weaving through the trees.
Whispers of a fleeting glance,
Carried on the gentle breeze.

Shadows play in golden hues,
Shapes that flicker, fade, and sway.
Caught between the sunlit views,
Life is but a fleeting ray.

Mystic forms in playful chase,
Tugging at the heart's desire.
A sunbeam's kiss, a warm embrace,
Fleeting dreams that spark a fire.

Elusive figures, lost and found,
In the light they twirl and spin.
Echoes linger all around,
Chasing joy, we're bound to win.

In the Realm of Vanishing Echoes

Echoes whisper through the trees,
A soft murmur, a fading song.
Carried on the evening breeze,
Where memories of dusk belong.

Shadows lengthen, night's embrace,
Fleeting moments from the day.
In this quiet, sacred space,
Whispers guide us on our way.

Voices soft, like mist in air,
Remnants of what once was near.
In the silence, we must dare,
To find the truth that's crystal clear.

Vanishing through the twilight's veil,
Echoes linger, soft yet strong.
In this realm, where dreams prevail,
We find courage to belong.

Fragments of Light Amidst the Dark

In the shadows, light will gleam,
Little sparks that pierce the night.
Fragments of a brighter dream,
Guiding us with tender light.

Stars above begin to glow,
Reminding us of what is true.
In the night, we learn to grow,
Finding hope in shades of blue.

Whispers of the past adore,
Echoes through the quiet air.
In the dark, we search for more,
Illuminated by a prayer.

Through the darkness, we will steer,
With each fragment, we ignite.
In the void, we conquer fear,
Creating warmth from tiny light.

Daydreams and Dappled Memories

In the garden of my mind,
Daydreams blossom, bright and free.
Dappled memories unwind,
Twisting through the shady tree.

Sunlight dances on the leaves,
Casting shadows, soft and warm.
Time, it flows, yet never leaves,
In this place, we find our charm.

Whispers of a bygone day,
Echo through the golden hour.
In these moments, drift away,
Wrapped in beauty, love's power.

Daydreams weave a timeless thread,
In the fabric of our minds.
Dappled memories softly spread,
In this haven, peace we find.

Haunting Remnants of a Day Gone By

The sun dips low, casting shadows long,
Whispers of twilight sing a soft song.
Memories dance on the edge of dark,
Holding the echoes of a fading spark.

Leaves rustle with secrets of hours spent,
A gentle breeze carries time's lament.
Moments captured in the twilight glow,
Lingering traces of what we used to know.

Stars emerge, each a glimmer of grace,
Reflecting the past in the night's embrace.
The moon holds vigil, a keeper of dreams,
As the world settles into silent streams.

In the stillness of night, our thoughts collide,
Haunting remnants of the day reside.
We tread softly through this endless maze,
Finding our peace in the softest gaze.

Journeying Through Daylight's Illusions

Under a sky so brilliantly blue,
We chase shadows that dance and skew.
Paths entwined in a labyrinth's weave,
Whispers of hope in the light we believe.

Mirages shimmer, yet truth lies beneath,
In each fleeting moment, sweet joy and grief.
With every step, we carve our own way,
In the symphony sung by the light of day.

Colors collide in a painter's dream,
Reality bends, or so it would seem.
Yet within the haze, a vision stays bright,
Guiding our hearts through the lingering light.

Journeying forth, we embrace the unknown,
Finding our place where the wild winds have blown.
Together we rise, through illusions we soar,
As daylight reveals what our souls must explore.

Light Threads Weaving Through the Aspirant's Mind

In the quiet dawn, thoughts start to bloom,
Threads of intention erase all the gloom.
Ideas glisten in the morning's embrace,
A tapestry forming in ethereal space.

Wisps of wisdom, elegant and fine,
Intertwining dreams in a sacred design.
Each thread a story, each hue a sign,
Captured within the transcendent divine.

As the day unfolds, visions ignite,
A symphony of colors dances in light.
The aspirant's heart finds solace, finds grace,
In the vibrant mural they passionately trace.

With every heartbeat, the woven threads grow,
Illuminating paths where courage will flow.
Light threads weaving through thoughts left unspun,
Unfolding the truths that can't be outdone.

Conversion of Thought into Light's Embrace

Thoughts like shadows whisper and tease,
Seeking the dawn, yearning for peace.
With each passing moment, ideas take flight,
Conversion begins in the soft morning light.

What once felt heavy sheds layers of care,
Illuminated wisdom flickers in air.
Light pours over doubts and fears that constrict,
Transforming the heart with a luminous script.

As dawn breaks forth, the shadows retreat,
Allowing the spirit to rise on its feet.
With love as our guide, we step into the glow,
Embracing the change, we let the storm go.

Conversion of thought into grace, into fire,
Becomes the foundation of dreams we aspire.
With every heartbeat, our spirits awake,
In light's warm embrace, we willingly break.

Echoes of a Bright Mirage

In the desert's hush, dreams rise anew,
Shadows play tricks in the shimmering view.
Waves of heat dance on amber sand,
Whispers of memories, a fleeting hand.

Mirages shimmer, elusive and bright,
Chasing the echoes in fading light.
Footsteps forgotten, a path without end,
Caught in the beauty no heart can defend.

The sun sinks low, painting skies with grace,
Each fading glow, a tender embrace.
In silence, we listen, the heartbeats sing,
A melody woven from everything.

Fleeting the vision, yet vivid and clear,
In dreams we wander, with nothing to fear.
Echoes of mirages, forever shall thrive,
In the crystal moments, we feel alive.

Illusions in the Golden Hour

When dusk caresses the horizon wide,
Illusions gather, the day's sweet pride.
Golden rays weave through branches like art,
Each fleeting moment steals a piece of heart.

Time holds its breath, the world feels surreal,
Colors burst forth, emotions reveal.
With each soft whisper, the shadows grow long,
In the heart of twilight, we find our song.

Embers of sunlight, a soft, tender glow,
Painted in layers, a gentle tableau.
Moments of magic, where dreams softly sway,
Illusions linger, then fade away.

As night creeps in, with stars in their chase,
The golden hour leaves but a trace.
We carry its glow, a warm, cherished light,
In memories held through the long, quiet night.

Stories Written in Soft Glows

Under the moonlight, tales come alive,
Each flicker of flame, a memory's drive.
Pages of dreams, unfolding the past,
Where whispers of night in our hearts are cast.

Soft glows illuminate paths untold,
Secrets and wishes in shades of gold.
With ink made of starlight and silver beams,
We write our stories in the thread of dreams.

In shadows they linger, these stories we weave,
Gentle reminders of all we believe.
Through the night's embrace, we search for signs,
In soft glows of solace, our spirit shines.

Moments suspended, where time stands still,
Crafting a narrative that echoes at will.
In every heartbeat, in every sigh,
Stories keep living as stars fill the sky.

The Dance of Illumination and Obscurity

In the twilight's sway, shadows do twirl,
Lights softly flicker, the night starts to whirl.
A ballet of contrasts, where darkness meets light,
In the dance of the moon, the world feels right.

Flickers of brilliance burst through the gray,
Illuminating hearts as they quietly play.
Each step a rhythm, both masking and bright,
A tapestry woven from day into night.

Obscurity whispers, its secrets secure,
Yet illumination draws us to explore.
In this delicate dance, we find our place,
Caught in the balance, a fragile embrace.

As night deepens further, each movement defines,
The essence of life that forever intertwines.
In the dance of existence, shadows take flight,
Illumination and obscurity, a wondrous sight.

Enigmas Wrapped in a Day's Embrace

Whispers dance under the sun's glow,
Secrets linger in the evening's flow.
Each moment holds a story untold,
Wrapped in warmth, the world unfolds.

Shadows stretch as twilight descends,
Curating tales as daylight ends.
In every heartbeat, a mystery lies,
In the depths of the shifting skies.

Footsteps echo on silent streets,
Fleeting faces in chance-filled meets.
Echoes of laughter, soft and near,
In the embrace of dusk, we steer.

The day dissolves into dreams' sway,
Enigmas linger—what will we say?
The night unfolds, a soft caress,
In shadows held, we find our rest.

The Mirage of Clarity

In the haze of thoughts that swirl around,
Truths elude where answers are found.
Every question leads to a fork,
In the silence, little sparks of talk.

Ripples swirl in the still of the mind,
Seeking visions that seem to rewind.
A mirage whispers of insights near,
Yet the more we chase, the more we fear.

Clouds obscure the brightening dawn,
Shadows dance where light is drawn.
Illusions flicker in the stare,
And clarity waits in the dusky air.

In fleeting moments, we strain to see,
Navigating through what cannot be.
Mirages play tricks on our weary quest,
In the heart's embrace, we find our rest.

Solaris and Shadows on the Cognizant Web

Threads of sunlight weave through the space,
Casting patterns, a revealing grace.
In this web, revelations glint,
A dance of shadows, where thoughts imprint.

Solaris reigns, igniting the night,
With whispers of wisdom, a guiding light.
Shadows curl like secrets long kept,
In the cradling arms where dreams leapt.

Cognizant moments twine and sway,
Capturing breath as night turns to day.
Each spark of thought in this woven seam,
Traces the outlines of a waking dream.

As light unfurls, the darkness breaks,
In the web of minds, new paths it makes.
We unravel stories in the twilight's hue,
Finding solace in the dance of the few.

Glimmers of What Could Be

In starlit nights where wishes fly,
Glimmers flicker, dreams in the sky.
Each thought released into the air,
Carries hopes for those who dare.

Mirrors of futures reflecting bright,
In the depths of the heart's soft light.
Every moment holds the key,
To unlock pathways, to what could be.

Eyes wide open, we seek and find,
Possibilities dance in the gentle wind.
With each breath, we shape our fate,
Crafting stories that won't hesitate.

Glimmers flicker, suspend disbelief,
As we journey toward endless relief.
In visions clear, may we always see,
The beauty of life and what could be.

Hidden Whispers Beneath Sunlit Canopies

In the forest deep, secrets hide,
Beneath leaves and branches, where shadows bide.
Gentle whispers drift on the breeze,
Carried softly through ancient trees.

Sunlight dapples the mossy floor,
Creating a canvas of legends and lore.
Each rustle and sigh holds a story untold,
In the heart of the woods, mysteries unfold.

Amidst the ferns, magic swells,
Nature's pulse, a symphony of spells.
Beneath the canopies, dreams intertwine,
Whispers of life, a rhythm divine.

Here, time pauses, and moments blend,
In hidden corners where echoes bend.
A sanctuary of thoughts, both bright and dim,
In the embrace of the trees, our spirits swim.

The Dance of Light and Elusion

Golden rays weave through the night,
Creating shadows, a mystical sight.
Footsteps twirl on a silken beam,
In a world where reality meets dream.

Soft glimmers play on the wall,
Illusions flicker, as whispers call.
Each twinkle holds a tale to share,
Of timeless dances, beyond compare.

Momentary glimpses, so rare to find,
The light leads on, uniting the blind.
In the silence of dusk, secrets unfold,
The dance of elusion, a mystery bold.

Lost in the rhythm of time's embrace,
We twirl with shadows, a waltz of grace.
In the flicker of stars, we take flight,
A journey ensues in the dance of light.

Radiant Echoes of a Wandering Spirit

Through valleys and hills, a spirit roams,
In search of the place where the heart calls home.
With every step, a memory gleams,
Reflecting the essence of long-lost dreams.

Echoes resonate in the twilight air,
A symphony woven with love and care.
In fallen leaves, whispers of grace,
The wandering spirit finds its place.

Stars guide the path through the silent night,
Illuminating shadows, igniting the light.
With courage as armor and hope as a shield,
The echoes of journeys are vividly revealed.

Each heartbeat dances with nature's own song,
In radiant moments where we all belong.
Wandering freely, with dreams that inspire,
The spirit ignites a never-ending fire.

Sunshine Trails and Mystic Paths

Along the trails where sunlight spills,
Lies a secret path that nature fills.
Whispers of magic in the golden glow,
Calling the seekers, as they softly go.

Beneath the arching trees so tall,
The air is thick with a soothing thrall.
Every turn unveils a hidden delight,
In the embrace of shadows, out of sight.

Mystic paths entwine with fate,
Each step a choice to contemplate.
In the rustling grass and the distant chime,
Time bends gently, suspended in rhyme.

Sunshine trails beckon all to explore,
Where the heart finds peace and yearns for more.
With every journey, we leave our mark,
On blissful trails that dance in the dark.

The Search for Essence in a Day's Glimmer

In morning's glow, the world awakes,
Soft whispers echo through the trees.
Each moment holds the essence still,
As sunlight dances on the leaves.

The shadows stretch, the colors blend,
A tapestry of light unfurls.
In fleeting time, we seek to grasp,
The magic of our earthly pearls.

With every breath, a story spun,
In shimmering hues, the day unfolds.
The search for essence never ends,
In glimmers bright, its truth beholds.

So journey forth, embrace the light,
For every dawn, a chance anew.
In day's glimmer, the heart will find,
The essence it has always knew.

Breaths of Sunlight in the Realm of Reverie

In realms where dreams and daylight meet,
Breaths of sunlight warm the soul.
Each flicker sparkles, bright and sweet,
A pathway to the heart's true goal.

The whispers swirl in soft embrace,
Through gardens where imagination roams.
In reverie, we find our place,
In golden hues, we craft our homes.

The lattice of our thoughts takes flight,
In every beam, a chance to soar.
With every shimmer, we ignite,
The magic that we can explore.

So let us linger in this space,
Where sunlight breathes through every dream.
In realms of reverie, we trace,
The threads of hope, a radiant seam.

Capturing the Flicker of a Thought's Flight

A thought takes wing upon the breeze,
It flutters gently, bright and bold.
In fleeting moments, time can tease,
As echoes of a dream unfold.

With every flicker, whispers call,
A glimpse of truth in shadows cast.
We chase the spark before it falls,
To seize the wisdom that will last.

In flight, the beauty of the mind,
Reflects the pulse of what we seek.
Capturing each glimmer we find,
We weave the tapestry unique.

So let us follow where it leads,
This flicker born from deep inside.
For in its wake lie hidden seeds,
Of dreams and hopes, our hearts confide.

Insights Blossoming in Radiant Spaces

In gardens lush, ideas bloom,
Petals unfurl in shades so bright.
Each insight's whisper clears the gloom,
Transforming shadows into light.

Among the leaves, wisdom hides,
Beneath the boughs of tranquil trees.
With every thought, a journey rides,
On currents carried by the breeze.

In radiant spaces, we can see,
The threads that weave our stories true.
Insights blossom, wild and free,
In every moment, painted hue.

So wander forth in search of grace,
Where beauty waits for hearts to find.
In radiant spaces, we embrace,
The insights of the open mind.

The Glow of Unseen Paths

In whispers soft, the shadows creep,
They guide us where the secrets sleep.
A shimmer glints on hidden trails,
As dreams take flight with gentle sails.

With every step, the heart will know,
The paths we choose, the ones that glow.
In quiet night, our spirits dance,
In twilight realms, we find our chance.

The glow ignites the darkest skies,
Illuminating what underlies.
With every choice, a spark is born,
Leading us to where we're worn.

Together bound, we'll trace the light,
A journey shared, our souls unite.
In unseen paths, we'll find our way,
With hope aglow, come what may.

Shifting Rays of Thoughtful Moments

In quiet hours, the mind will roam,
Through shifting rays, we find our home.
Thoughts like clouds, they drift and sway,
Casting shadows, brightening day.

With each reflection, new colors blend,
In thoughtful moments, we can mend.
Beneath the surface, ideas bloom,
In subtle light, dispelling gloom.

A fleeting glance, a knowing smile,
In shifting rays, we pause awhile.
Time holds breath in fragile grace,
Each moment etched, we must embrace.

So let us savor, cherish deep,
These shifting rays that help us leap.
For in the light, we see the best,
Transforming thought, igniting quest.

Beyond the Spectrum of Perception

In realms unseen, the colors sing,
A vibrant dance of everything.
Beyond the eyes, a world unfolds,
In spectrum bright, the soul beholds.

With every glance, a truth we find,
In shadows cast, the light is kind.
A myriad hues, both bold and faint,
Reveal the heart, a canvas quaint.

Through subtle whispers, vision grows,
Beyond the limits, beauty flows.
In every shade, a story spun,
A tapestry where dreams are won.

So let us seek, beyond the view,
In every tone, a path so true.
For in this light, we come to see,
The spectrum wide, we long to be.

Glints of Possibility in the Clear

In morning's breath, the world awakes,
With glints of hope that softly shakes.
Each moment holds a hidden spark,
Illuminating the once-dark park.

With eyes attuned to skies so blue,
Possibilities form, ever new.
In glimmers bright, we find our flight,
A journey awaits, the soul's delight.

Each choice we make, a step we take,
In clear horizons, dreams we stake.
With hearts aligned to what we seek,
The future gleams, both bold and meek.

So let us cherish each small clue,
In glints of light, our paths accrue.
For in the clear, we'll rise and soar,
Embracing all, forevermore.

Phantoms Woven from Day's Warmth

In the cradle of twilight, they linger soft,
Shadows of laughter, where dreams take off.
Gentle whispers echo in the fading light,
Woven from moments that feel just right.

Carried by breezes, they softly sway,
Calling to hearts that have lost their way.
Threads of the past in a tapestry spun,
Phantoms of joy in the setting sun.

Restless they dance, by the river's bend,
Memories flicker, like starlight's blend.
Chasing the dusk, they twirl and spin,
Crafted by warmth, where our tales begin.

In every heartbeat, they come alive,
Together we wander, where phantoms thrive.
Softly they beckon, through fields of gold,
Whispers of stories, forever told.

The Glow of Memories in Sunlit Strolls

Through fields of daisies, we walk as one,
Each step a spark, beneath the sun.
Laughter lingers in the warm, bright air,
A dance of shadows, a moment rare.

Sunlight filters through the whispering leaves,
Painting our journey as daylight weaves.
Golden paths lead where time stands still,
Captured in fragments, a heart to fill.

Softly we reminisce of days gone by,
Under the canvas of a cerulean sky.
With every glance, the past comes alive,
In the glow of memories, we learn to thrive.

Hand in hand, we trace what we find,
Shadows of laughter, in the heart and mind.
Sunlit strolls linger, like echoes of song,
In the garden of moments where we belong.

Whispering Winds in the Fields of Bright Thoughts

A gentle breeze stirs the golden grain,
Whispering secrets only hearts can explain.
Fields alive with colors, vivid and bright,
Echoes of laughter, dancing in the light.

Thoughts like wildflowers, in soft shades bloom,
Caressing the air, dispelling the gloom.
In the embrace of nature, freedom sings,
As whispering winds carry joyful wings.

With every rustle, a story unfolds,
Promising tales that the heart beholds.
In these vast fields, where dreams take flight,
Whispering winds lead us toward the light.

Close your eyes, feel the warmth and the grace,
Find solace in movement, in time and space.
In the fields of bright thoughts, let spirits soar,
With every gust, we're forever more.

Shadows Dispersed in the Dance of Light

Dancing on edges where daylight plays,
Shadows retreat in the sun's warm rays.
Glimmers of hope in a world so wide,
Together we step, with nothing to hide.

In the ballet of dusk, they twirl and glide,
Merging with colors where visions reside.
Holding the promise of a new dawn's plight,
Shadows dispersed in the dance of light.

Every heartbeat echoes, a rhythm divine,
Flowing like water, in soft, perfect line.
Lifting us higher, on winds that ignite,
Shadows dispersed in the dance of light.

Here in the twilight, we find our peace,
In the tender embrace, our worries cease.
Together we shimmer, like stars in the night,
Living as one in this dance of light.

Silhouettes Dancing in Day's Embrace

In daylight's glow, shadows arise,
They twist and turn beneath the skies.
Whispers of dreams in the light's warm haze,
Silhouettes dance in the sun's soft gaze.

Their forms entwined in a graceful sway,
A ballet of light that invites the day.
With every movement, stories unfold,
In this fleeting moment, a tale retold.

The trees lean close, sharing their song,
As the sun plays softly, it won't be long.
To capture this beauty, we only need,
A heart that listens, a soul to heed.

In daylight's embrace, we find our muse,
In shadows and light, we can't refuse.
Together we dance, forever we stay,
In the warmth of the sun, come what may.

Fleeting Figures Under the Sun's Gaze

Figures fleeting, moving fast,
Beneath the sun, shadows are cast.
With laughter and joy, they skip and twirl,
Like petals caught in a wild world.

Each moment a spark in the golden light,
Chasing echoes, a breathtaking sight.
Upon the pavement, dreams collide,
In this dance, we all confide.

Time slips away, like grains of sand,
In the warmth of the sun, we stand hand in hand.
Life's little joys, like whispers shared,
Fleeting figures, forever paired.

Under the sun's gaze, shadows may fade,
But memories linger, never betrayed.
In the dance of the day, we know we're alive,
In this moment of magic, we thrive.

Sunbeams and Elusive Fantasies

Sunbeams scatter like dreams on the run,
Chasing the light, we bask in the fun.
Elusive fantasies, bright and bold,
Whispering secrets that never grow old.

With laughter we weave through the rays we chase,
In the warmth of the sun, we find our place.
A flicker of hope in the afternoon glow,
In this jubilant dance, we let our hearts flow.

The world falls away, just you and I,
Under the sky where the sun yet flies.
Together we dream, in colors so bright,
In the sunbeam's embrace, we take our flight.

As shadows stretch long and daylight fades,
We hold these moments, no need for charades.
Elusive, yet vivid, our fantasies shine,
In a world crafted solely by time.

Illusions of Laughter in Sunlit Reverie

In the golden glow, laughter appears,
Illusions of joy that drown out our fears.
With every giggle, a story takes flight,
In whispers of laughter, hearts feel light.

Sunlit reverie, a dream in the day,
Where moments linger, and worries sway.
Between the rays, we find our tune,
A melody played in the afternoon.

Through fields of daisies, our spirits roam,
In the light of the sun, we feel at home.
Each smile is painted in colors so clear,
A canvas of hope, forever near.

As twilight falls and the laughter fades,
We treasure the echoes, the joyful cascades.
In our sunlit dreams, we'll always reside,
With illusions of laughter forever our guide.

The Pursuit of Glimmering Echoes

In the shadows, whispers play,
Chasing dreams that fade away.
Footsteps on a silent street,
Heartbeats quicken with each beat.

Echoes dance in twilight's gleam,
Fleeting moments, lost in dream.
Searching for a touch of light,
Guided by the stars so bright.

Time slips through like grains of sand,
Wishes written in the land.
Fragments of a life once lived,
All our secrets laid and sieved.

Glimmers sparkle in the night,
Shimmering in soft moonlight.
With each step, we find our way,
To the dawn of a new day.

Twilight Reflections on a Bright Canvas

Colors merge in dusky skies,
Painting visions, soft and wise.
Brushstrokes weave a tale of time,
In the silence, thoughts do chime.

Mirrored skies on tranquil seas,
Whispers carried by the breeze.
Horizons stretch, alive and true,
Beneath the hues of purple blue.

Stars awaken, one by one,
As the day has now been spun.
Night's embrace, a gentle sigh,
Cradles dreams that learn to fly.

In this moment, life stands still,
Hearts entwined with fate's sweet thrill.
Twilight's dance, a fleeting glance,
In the canvas of our chance.

Flickers of Hope in a Luminous World

In valleys deep and mountains high,
Where shadows lurk and spirits sigh.
Flickers dart like fireflies,
Painting hope across the skies.

A single spark ignites the dark,
Warming hearts with just a spark.
Threads of light weave through the pain,
Binding souls like summer rain.

With each whisper, hope returns,
Igniting dreams with gentle yearns.
A radiant glow against the night,
Guiding every lost soul's flight.

In this world where shadows creep,
Flickers of hope stir from sleep.
Together, we'll find our way,
Chasing dawn of a new day.

Beneath the Brilliance of Daylight's Veil

Sunlight dances on the grass,
Every moment, fleeting pass.
Underneath the azure sky,
Nature whispers soft and shy.

Flowers bloom with vibrant cheer,
In the warmth, the world draws near.
Colors burst, a feast for eyes,
Joyful laughter fills the skies.

With every beam of golden glow,
Life awakens, spirits flow.
Underneath the daylight's rhyme,
Dreams arise, transcending time.

Together, we embrace the light,
Promising to hold on tight.
Beneath the brilliance, hearts reveal,
The gentle magic we can feel.

Pursuing the Light of Hidden Thoughts

In the shadows, whispers stir,
Silent secrets that we infer.
Glimmers dance in the dark's embrace,
Chasing echoes of a forgotten place.

Flickers of hope, so soft and slight,
Guiding us through the veil of night.
A journey mapped in our restless minds,
Where every truth patiently unwinds.

As dawn breaks, the shadows flee,
Revealing dreams, wild and free.
In each thought, a spark ignites,
Pursuing the glow of hidden lights.

With every step, we seek, we crave,
Understanding what hearts might save.
In the whispers, visions take flight,
Pursuing the light of hidden thoughts.

Specters of Dreams in Bright Horizons

In twilight's clutch, we dare to dream,
Specters rise like a silver beam.
Each horizon glows with untold tales,
Where hope and wonder set their trails.

Colors swirl in a vivid dance,
Visions tease, ignite romance.
Floating gently on the breeze,
Dreams unfold with graceful ease.

Beyond the strife, the light draws near,
Whispers of joy for those who hear.
In the spectrum, futures gleam,
Specters of our deepest dreams.

Together we chase, hand in hand,
To realms where spirits freely stand.
In bright horizons, we find our way,
Guided by the dreams we sway.

Racing Through Radiance

Through fields of gold, we swiftly run,
Chasing rays of a blinding sun.
Each heartbeat syncs with the vibrant light,
Racing forward, hearts take flight.

Laughter echoes like a sweet refrain,
As we dance through the gentle rain.
Radiance sparkles on our skin,
A symphony of joy begins.

With every step, the world ignites,
In a whirlwind of brilliant sights.
Together we weave a tapestry bright,
Racing through the boundless light.

As twilight whispers, we won't yield,
Our dreams like banners unsealed.
In this moment, we find our place,
Racing through radiance, with grace.

Echoes of Light in the Heart's Garden

In the garden where silence blooms,
Echoes linger, dispelling glooms.
Petals fall like whispered sighs,
Bathing the earth in soft replies.

A dance of shadows, light unfolds,
In secrets shared, a tale retold.
With every ray, the blossom gleams,
Fragrant whispers of our dreams.

As twilight gathers, colors blend,
The heart's garden begins to mend.
In radiant hues, we find our way,
Echoes of light guide us each day.

Through gentle breezes, love will soar,
In our souls, forevermore.
In this haven, we grow and start,
Echoes of light in the heart's garden.